CONTENTS

Words in the glossary appear in **bold** type the first time they are used in the text.

CONNECTING CANAL

The Panama Canal is a man-made waterway in Central America. It connects the Atlantic Ocean and the Pacific Ocean. It's about 40 miles (64 km) long from shore to shore. Many ocean trade routes, or paths, were much longer before the Panama Canal was built.

THE PANAMA CANAL

BY MARIE ROESSER

Gareth Stevens PUBLISHING

CRASHCOURSE

Please visit our website, www.garethstevens.com. For a free color catalog of all our high-quality books, call toll free 1-800-542-2595 or fax 1-877-542-2596.

Library of Congress Cataloging-in-Publication Data

Names: Roesser, Marie, author.
Title: The Panama Canal / Marie Roesser.
Description: New York : Gareth Stevens Publishing, [2020] | Series: A look at U.S. history | Includes index.
Identifiers: LCCN 2019014321| ISBN 9781538248799 (pbk.) | ISBN 9781538248812 (library bound) | ISBN 9781538248805 (6 pack)
Subjects: LCSH: Panama Canal (Panama)--History.
Classification: LCC F1569.C2 R64 2020 | DDC 97.287/5--dc23
LC record available at https://lccn.loc.gov/2019014321

First Edition

Published in 2020 by
Gareth Stevens Publishing
111 East 14th Street, Suite 349
New York, NY 10003

Editor: Therese Shea

Photo credits: Series art Christophe BOISSON/Shutterstock.com; (feather quill) Galushko Sergey/Shutterstock.com; (parchment) mollicart-design/Shutterstock.com; cover, pp. 1, 15 Everett Historical/Shutterstock.com; p. 5 Will & Deni McIntyre/ The Image Bank/Getty Images Plus/Getty Images; p. 7 dikobraziy/Shutterstock.com; p. 9 Print Collector/ Hulton Archive/Getty Images; p. 11 Courtesy of the Library of Congress; p. 13 Photo 12/ Universal Images Group/Getty Images; p. 17 Bettmann/Getty Images; p. 19 Buyenlarge/Archive Photos/Getty Images; p. 21 Galina Savina/Shutterstock.com; p. 23 DEA/A. DAGLI ORTI/ De Agostini/Getty Images; p. 25 Yingna Cai/Shutterstock.com; p. 27 Diego Grandi/ Shutterstock.com; p. 29 Andreea Dragomir/Shutterstock.com.

Printed in the United States of America

CPSIA compliance information: Batch #CW20GS: For further information contact Gareth Stevens, New York, New York at 1-800-542-2595.

MAKE THE GRADE

A canal is a long narrow path made by people that's filled with water. It's used for boat travel and to bring water to or from a place.

BEFORE THE CANAL

Before the Panama Canal, boats traveling between New York City and San Francisco, California, went around the tip of South America. This was a trip about 13,000 miles (20,921 km) long. Using the canal cut the trip to about 5,000 miles (8,047 km).

SAN FRANCISCO

NEW YORK CITY

5,000 MILES

13,000 MILES

MAKE THE GRADE

The canal also makes the trip shorter for vessels, or ships, carrying goods between Europe and the west coast of the Americas as well as East Asia.

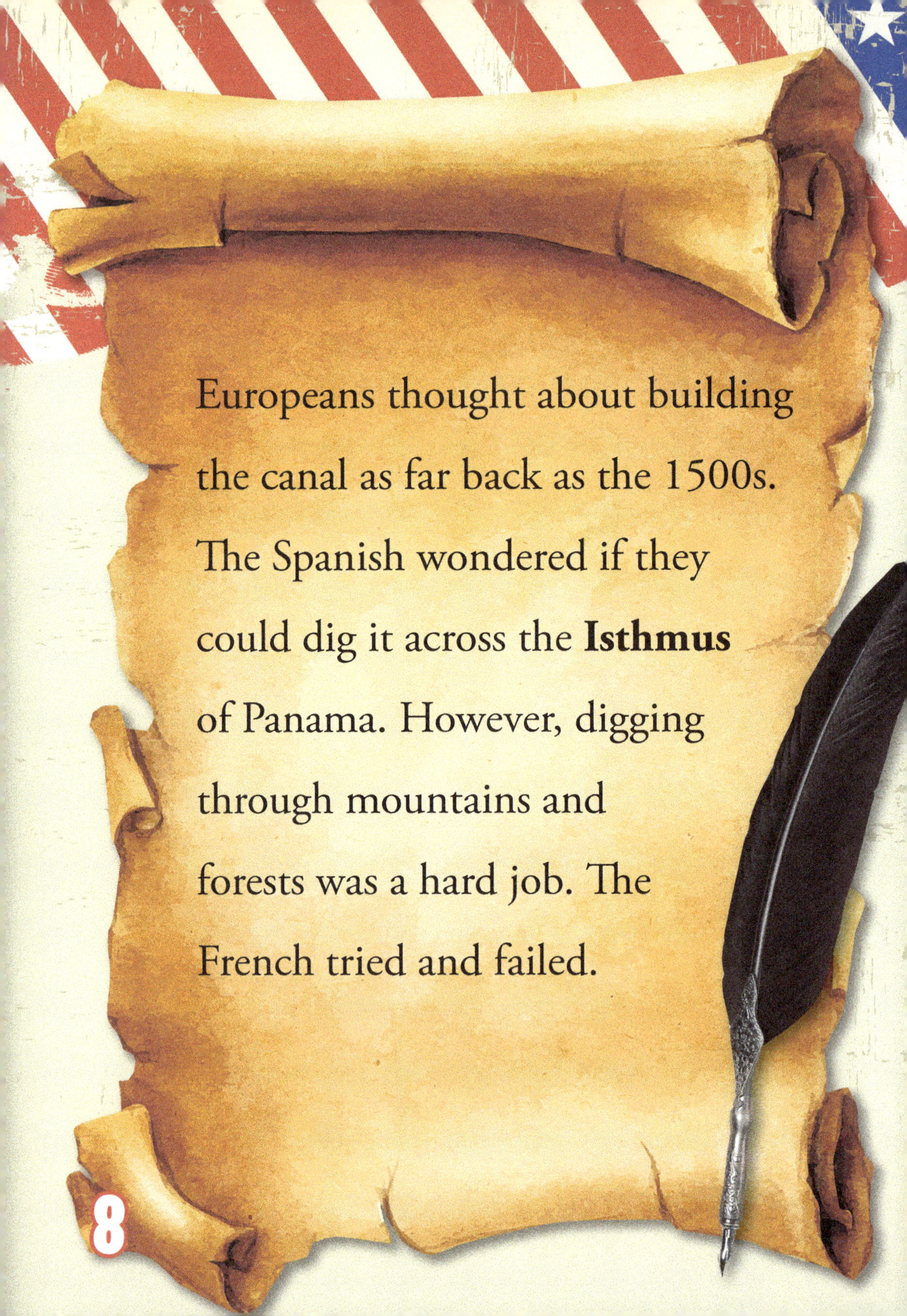

Europeans thought about building the canal as far back as the 1500s. The Spanish wondered if they could dig it across the **Isthmus** of Panama. However, digging through mountains and forests was a hard job. The French tried and failed.

MAKE THE GRADE

The French tried to build a canal in the late 1800s. They gave up because of diseases, or illnesses, and other problems. About 22,000 workers died.

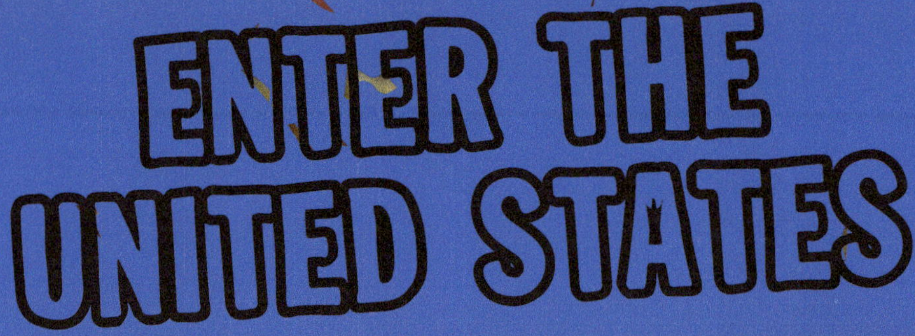

ENTER THE UNITED STATES

In 1902, the United States decided to take over the canal where France left off. However, the land where the canal would be built belonged to Colombia. The Colombian government wouldn't agree to sell the land to the United States.

MAKE THE GRADE

The United States and England had planned to dig a canal through Nicaragua, but it was never built.

A REVOLUTION

Some Colombians were angered by their government's **decision**. They decided to have a **revolution**. US president Theodore Roosevelt sent armed forces to help. The country of Panama was formed. The new government let the United States buy the land for the canal.

MAKE THE GRADE

The United States agreed to pay Panama $10 million for the canal land plus $250,000 for the use of the canal every year after.

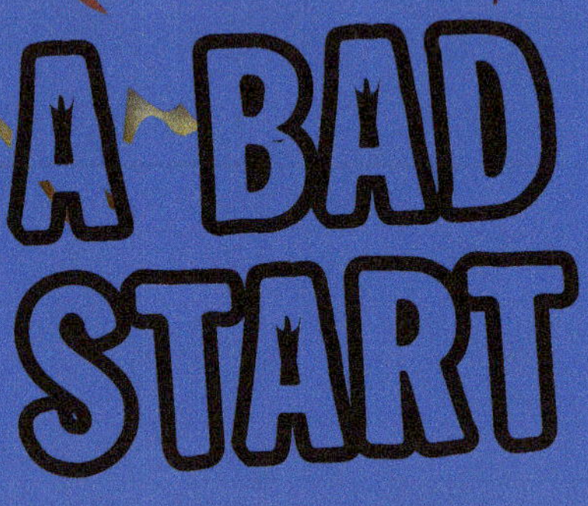

At first, canal **construction** looked like it would fail. The tools the United States had bought from France didn't work well. Worse, many workers became sick with the diseases **yellow fever** and **malaria**. The chief **engineer** quit after a year.

MAKE THE GRADE

Around the time of the canal's construction, people discovered malaria and yellow fever spread through the bite of the bugs called mosquitos.

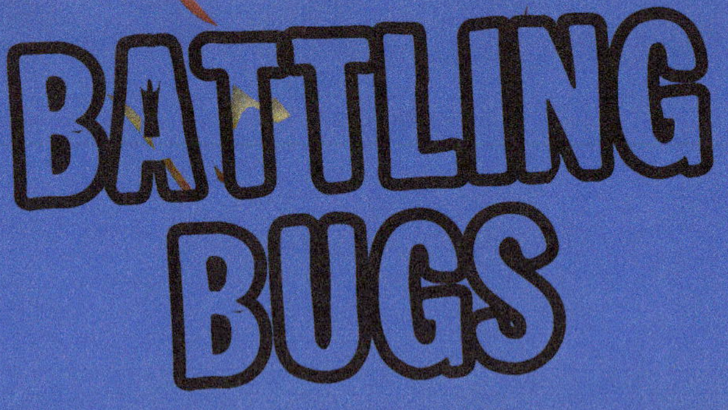

BATTLING BUGS

US army doctor William Gorgas led the battle against disease. Mosquitoes lay eggs in still bodies of water. So, Gorgas had the water taken out of ponds and lakes. He made sure houses and buildings had **screens**. New hospitals were built as well.

MAKE THE GRADE

The cases of yellow fever and malaria dropped sharply because of Gorgas's plan.

THE BIG DIG

With healthy workers, the real construction could begin. Some worked with shovels. Others used **cranes**, drills, and **dynamite**. Huge machines dug into the earth and lifted dirt into railroad cars, which took the dirt away. **Concrete** was poured within the canal's locks.

MAKE THE GRADE

Landslides, floods, and an **earthquake** added to the trouble of building the Panama Canal.

LOCK STEPS

Locks were built at certain points along the canal. They work like steps. When a boat moves into a lock, gates close. Water comes in or out to raise or lower the boat. Then, the boat moves to the next lock.

MAKE THE GRADE

Around the middle of the locks is a man-made body of water called Gatún Lake. It's more than 80 feet (24 m) above sea level, or the average height of the surface of Earth's oceans.

CONSTRUCTION COMPLETE

On October 10, 1913, President Woodrow Wilson pressed a button in the White House, about 4,000 miles (6,437 km) from the Panama Canal. That made a flood of water rush into the canal. The canal opened August 15, 1914.

MAKE THE GRADE

The canal had cost about $380 million. It was the most costly construction job in US history at that time.

WHERE THE WATER COMES FROM

The Panama Canal uses a huge amount of water. Its locks need about 48 million gallons (182 million l) of water for each vessel. Most of this water comes from Gatún Lake. A dam at one end of the Chagres River created this lake.

MAKE THE GRADE

The canal locks work today with the help of computers and cameras.

WAITING FOR A TURN

About 40 vessels go through the canal each day. The trip takes between 8 and 10 hours. Big ships often pay tens of thousands of dollars or more to go through. Sometimes they wait days for their turn through the canal.

MAKE THE GRADE

American Richard Halliburton paid 36 cents to swim the Panama Canal in 1928!

A WORLD WONDER

The United States gave control of the canal to Panama in 1999. New construction has allowed very large ships packed with goods to pass through. The Panama Canal changed world travel. It's called one of the seven wonders of the modern world!

MAKE THE GRADE

About 14,000 vessels use the canal each year. Over 1 million ships have passed through it so far.

TIMELINE OF THE PANAMA CANAL

1882
France begins building a canal in today's Panama.

1889
France gives up on digging the canal.

1902
The United States decides to take over the unfinished canal.

1903
A revolution in Colombia ends in a newly formed country—Panama.

1904
The United States buys control of the canal land from Panama and prepares to dig.

1905
After more than a year of fighting disease, the last case of yellow fever is reported near the canal.

1909
Construction begins on locks.

1914
The canal opens August 15.

1999
The United States gives control of the canal to Panama.

2016
A third set of locks is completed in the Panama Canal for more ships to pass through.

GLOSSARY

concrete: a hard, strong matter used for building and made by mixing cement, sand, and broken rocks with water

construction: having to do with the act of building something

crane: a machine with a long arm used for lifting and moving heavy objects

decision: a choice made after thinking about something

dynamite: a powerful explosive, which is matter that causes a great blast

earthquake: a shaking of the ground caused by the movement of Earth's crust

engineer: one who plans and builds machines

isthmus: a narrow piece of land that connects two larger pieces of land

landslide: the sudden movement of rocks and dirt down a hill or mountain

malaria: an illness that causes chills and fever and is passed from one person to another by mosquito bites

revolution: a movement to overthrow a government

screen: thin pieces of wire or cloth put over windows to keep bugs out

yellow fever: an illness that causes fever and yellowish skin that can be passed from one person to another through mosquito bites

FOR MORE INFORMATION

Books

Currie, Stephen. *The Panama Canal.* San Diego, CA: ReferencePoint Press, 2015.

LaPierre, Yvette. *Engineering the Panama Canal.* Minneapolis, MN: Core Library, 2018.

Websites

How It Works

www.pancanal.com/eng/general/howitworks/

Watch a video to see how the canal works.

US History: Panama Canal

www.ducksters.com/history/us_1900s/panama_canal.php

Read a short history of the canal.

Publisher's note to educators and parents: Our editors have carefully reviewed these websites to ensure that they are suitable for students. Many websites change frequently, however, and we cannot guarantee that a site's future contents will continue to meet our high standards of quality and educational value. Be advised that students should be closely supervised whenever they access the internet.

INDEX